Country Walks in
SURREY

15 leisurely rambles

David Weller

COUNTRYSIDE BOOKS
NEWBURY BERKSHIRE

First published 2010
© David Weller 2010

COUNTRYSIDE BOOKS
3 Catherine Road
Newbury, Berkshire

To view our complete range of books,
please visit us at
www.countrysidebooks.co.uk

ISBN 978 1 84674 178 4

Maps and photographs by the author

Designed by Peter Davies, Nautilus Design
Produced through MRM Associates Ltd., Reading
Printed in Thailand

Contents

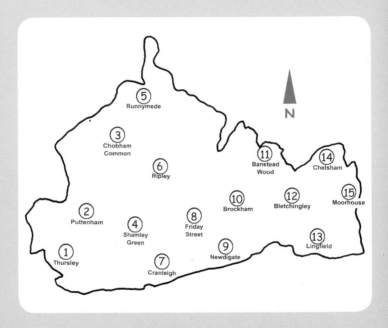

■ *Area map showing location of the walks* ■

Introduction

At the forefront of my mind whilst devising these enjoyable circular walks were those people who would much prefer to set a leisurely pace that allows plenty of time for the discovery of interesting flora and fauna, or the history and architecture of the area they are passing through, maybe topped off with a picnic along the way.

A slower pace is often rewarded with sightings of wildlife, whether pheasants at the field edge, trout in a shady pool or deer grazing. A closer inspection of the hedgerow may lead to the discovery of interesting lichen, wildflowers or fungi that would not be spotted at a faster pace. After all, there are other books for those who wish to march off through the countryside with the aim of achieving a great mileage in a short time.

Some of my walks contain a hill or two but to exclude these circuits would do a great disservice to the county and they will not trouble the average person; just take your time and remember it's not a race. Many routes are ideal for picnicking, so why not pack a sandwich and a drink into your haversack and enjoy lunch alfresco?

I always recommend walking boots as they offer grip in mud and support on uneven ground. My sketch maps are drawn to scale and to make following them easier, they also contain numbers that correspond to each paragraph of my text, but for a better overview of the circuits I have recommended the relevant Ordnance Survey map at the beginning of each route.

So, enjoy these easy walks and remember, the longer you take the more of interest you will see!

Publisher's Note

We hope that you obtain considerable enjoyment from this book; great care has been taken in its preparation. Although at the time of publication all routes followed public rights of way or permitted paths, diversion orders can be made and permissions withdrawn.

We cannot, of course, be held responsible for such diversion orders and any inaccuracies in the text which result from these or any other changes to the routes, nor any damage which might result from walkers trespassing on private property. We are anxious though that all details covering the walks are kept up to date and would therefore welcome information from readers which would be relevant to future editions.

The simple sketch maps that accompany the walks in this book are based on notes made by the author whilst checking out the routes on the ground. They are designed to show you how to reach the start, to point out the main features of the overall circuit and they contain a progression of numbers that relate to the paragraphs of the text.

However, for the benefit of a proper map, we do recommend that you purchase the relevant Ordnance Survey sheet covering your walk. The Ordnance Survey maps are widely available, especially through booksellers and local newsagents.

1

Thursley, Houndown and The Moat

■ *Water lilies on The Moat* ■

If it's peace and tranquility you seek, then you can do no better than walk this great circuit. As the route leaves Thursley village it passes along a delightful lane lined by 16th-century houses before continuing through the manicured grounds of Dye House to reach the wilds of Houndown. Here the route

Country Walks in Surrey

Distance: 4 miles

Starting point: Car park by the village cricket pitch.
GR 899398

How to get there: Thursley is 9 miles south of Guildford
and 1 mile west of the A3. From the A3, pass the Three
Horseshoes pub and the tiny triangular village green and
park in the car park beside the cricket pitch.

OS Map: Landranger 186 Aldershot & Guildford

Refreshments: The Three Horseshoes, or picnic at
The Moat.

follows a little-used track bordered by peaceful woodland where the
only sound to break the silence is birdsong. As it begins its return, it
passes the bank of The Moat where you may wish to picnic and while
away some time watching the waterfowl. To complete the circuit, the
route follows sandy tracks beside Thursley Nature Reserve before
rejoining the village.

The Walk

❶ From the car park, walk back to the triangular village green and
turn sharp right along **The Lane** passing ancient houses. When
the road ends, continue ahead on a well-trodden path through
woodland and keep left at a fork to soon meet a road. Turn left
along the road and immediately after passing **Horn Cottage**, turn
left on a private drive. In 120 yards cross a stile on your right,
continue over a brook and follow a low fence through the grounds
of unseen **Dye House** where after climbing a rise and crossing a
second bridge a road is met.

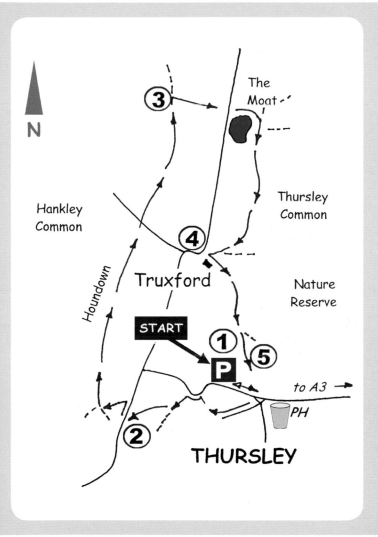

■ *A pretty path through the woodland* ■

❷ Turn right alongside the road for 150 yards before turning left into **Houndown Lane**. Follow the lane when it bends right and press on with peaceful woodland on your right and the wilds of **Hankley Common** to your left. After almost 1 mile, a tarmac lane crosses the track and here you should continue ahead passing a gate. Later pass a few well-appointed houses to reach the ornate gates of **Elstead Manor** in ½ mile.

❸ Turn right here on a wide path through woodland to reach a road. Cross to a car park opposite and make your way to the bank of **The Moat** which is a good picnic spot. Turn left along the bank following **Heath Trail** signs which soon bring you to a crossing path by a **Thursley National Nature Reserve** sign. *Although our way is right here, you may wish to investigate the boardwalk ahead of you that leads through Thursley Bog where, depending on the time of the year, you will see marsh orchids, the insectivorous sundew and myriads of dragonflies in this unusual landscape.* From this sign, turn right on a wide sandy path that borders the dry heathland of the nature reserve. Later keep right at a fork to meet a T junction in 150 yards. Turn right here to reach a bridleway joining from the left with a road 35 yards ahead of you.

❹ Turn hard left here onto the joining bridleway and pass by a gate and a house. The bridleway now follows the edge of a field on your right and you should ignore paths forking left. At the end of the field by a marker post, our way forks left on the signed bridleway where you should ignore a crossing path.

❺ Pass a second marker post and continue ahead at a third on a narrow path between trees ignoring a crossing track in 25 yards while a further 25 yards brings you to a T-junction. Turn right now and pass to the left of a cottage to meet the triangular village green where to your right will be found the car park and the end of this good walk.

2

Puttenham Common and The Tarn

■ *The Tarn marks the halfway point of the walk* ■

This pleasurable walk begins by following a section of the North Downs Way from the village to meet Puttenham Common where a track passes through a gorgeous blend of heath and peaceful woodland. Soon the route strikes out across the common to meet the halfway point at the bank of The Tarn, a

Distance: 5 miles

Starting point: The Street in Puttenham village
GR 930478

How to get there: Puttenham is 4 miles west of
Guildford. Follow the signs from the A31 Hog's Back dual
carriageway and park at the roadside in The Street just
west of the Good Intent pub.

OS Map: Landranger 186 Aldershot & Guildford

Refreshments: The Good Intent pub in The Street,
or picnic along the route.

serene lake set amongst pine woodland. Continuing on, the way goes round the end of Cutt Mill Pond before passing 17th-century Rodsall Manor as it heads for the most popular part of the common where panoramic views and a picnic spot are an attraction. From here the route continues on a wide track before crossing a couple of fields to join a scenic lane leading back to the village.

The Walk

❶ Walk westwards along **The Street** and at its junction with **Seale Lane**, go ahead on **Lascombe Lane** passing **Highfield Lane** in 150 yards. At the lane's end, continue ahead on a well-trodden path signed as the **North Downs Way** long-distance path and remain on it with views of the **Hog's Back** to your right.

■ *A distant view from the North Downs Way* ■

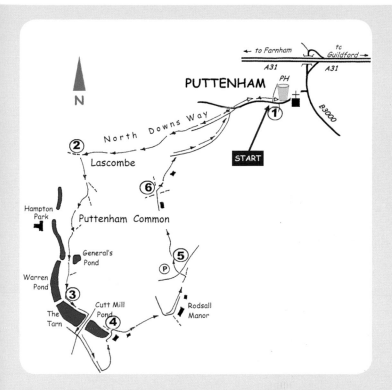

② After ¾ mile a small rough parking area is met and here we leave the long-distance path by turning left through woodland on a bridleway. Note the low wire fence on your right because for the next mile our path never strays far from it. At a fork, keep right and 90 yards later, fork right again and ignore any paths to your left. After rounding a bend and climbing a rise to meet a T-junction, turn right and press on to the top of the hill. Continue on the down slope and after passing **General's Pond** ignore a left fork in the track to reach the bank of **The Tarn**.

3 The circuit continues left along the water's edge and meets with a country lane. Turn right along the lane passing the end of **The Tarn** to reach a road junction in 150 yards. Go left on the road signed to **Shackleford** and 50 yards before a house is reached on the left, go left on a signed bridleway. In 20 yards, ignore a left fork and remain on the well-signed bridleway through woodland. When it joins a wide track, go ahead and in 85 yards follow the bridleway right to pass between **Cutt Mill Pond** and 17th-century **Cutt Mill House** to meet a driveway.

4 Turn right along the drive and when it ends, continue ahead on the bridleway which will finally bring you to a drive where you should turn right ignoring a bridleway signed rightwards on a bend. Pass by ancient **Rodsall Manor** and continue ahead between farm buildings. Soon pass **Rose Cottage** where the bridleway continues between banks and look out for a left turn up steps where you skirt a garden to meet a road.

5 Cross the road and go ahead on a bridleway to the right of a height barrier at **Puttenham Common Top** car park. Pass an open picnic area with panoramic views and at a line of low posts bear right and go through a dip forking right to meet a track. Turn left along the track passing a large house to meet a junction of tracks 100 yards later.

6 Go ahead for 20 yards before forking right through a kissing gate and passing through **Lascombe Wood** on a well-trodden path. Leave the woodland via a fenced path, pass a house and go over a stile ahead of you. Maintain direction over a paddock crossing a stile at the far side and continue over an arable field to meet a quiet lane. Turn right along the lane to eventually join **Lascombe Lane** and our outward path. Turn right and soon continue ahead along **The Street** to complete this good circuit.

3

Chobham Common and Oystershell Hill

■ *Much of the route is along wide sandy tracks* ■

This lovely heathland route leads you along wide sandy tracks that cross the wilds of Chobham Common, an important National Nature Reserve that supports a good variety of flora and fauna. The walk begins by crossing Albury Bottom on a track that offers easy walking and panoramic views. As the

Distance: 3¼ miles

Starting point: Longcross car park at the junction of Staple Hill and Longcross Road. GR 979651

How to get there: From Chobham High Street, go north along Windsor Road (B383) and in 1¾ miles fork right into Staple Hill. The car park will be found on your right at the junction with Longcross Road (B386) in 1¼ miles.

OS Map: Landranger 176 West London

Refreshments: There are eateries and coffee shops in Chobham, or picnic on the route.

way turns and begins to head back, it follows a well-trodden path through woodland and around the foot of Chickabiddy Hill before passing under the M3 motorway to continue over open heath. The route then follows a wide track that skirts the twin hillocks of Oystershell Hill before all too soon ending back at the car park.

The Walk

❶ Leave the car park on a track opposite the entrance and take the right fork when it divides after 100 yards. Now remain on this lovely track as it crosses **Albury Bottom** and heads for power cables in the distance. As you near the power cables the track forks 20 yards before a single pine tree. Take the right fork to meet a T-junction in 100 yards.

❷ Turn right, and continue through woodland where you will soon notice a scrap yard through the trees to your right. At the end of the yard, turn right on a well-trodden path between trees to join a

■ *The track across Albury Bottom* ■

driveway where you should continue ahead to meet a road. Cross the road and follow a narrow bridleway opposite that rises gently through woodland. At the top of the slope pass under power cables, ignore a smaller path that forks left and remain on the main path to meet a wide crossing track below the oddly-named **Chickabiddy Hill**.

❸ Turn right here and ignore side paths. Some 70 yards before a height barrier and a road are reached, turn sharp left on a bridleway

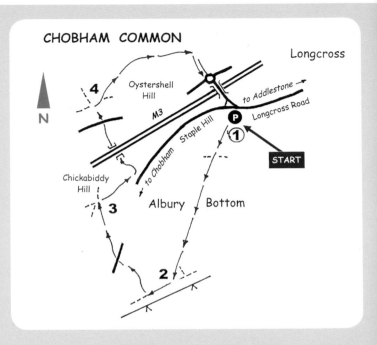

CHOBHAM COMMON

Longcross

Oystershell Hill

to Addlestone →

Longcross Road

M3

Staple Hill

P

(1)

START

to Chobham

Chickabiddy Hill

Albury

Bottom

3

4

N

2

that leads to a tunnel under the M3 motorway. Continue through the tunnel and keep ahead to meet a road. Go ahead on the bridleway opposite to meet a wide crossing track in 180 yards.

4 Turn right here and remain on the wide track as it skirts to the left of the twin hillocks of **Oystershell Hill**. Ignore side paths and remain on the main track that finally enters a tree line, passes a seat and ends at a disused road. Turn right along the road; pass a unique height barrier for horse riders to soon meet a roundabout. Press on ahead, cross a bridge over the M3 and pass the end of a road signed to **Chobham** to rejoin **Longcross** car park to complete this good circuit.

4

Shamley Green, the Wey-South and Downs Link paths

■ *The trackbed of the old railway offers easy walking* ■

This superb circuit begins beside the village duck pond before joining a section of the Greensand Way which leads you over fields with panoramic views. After passing through a pretty bluebell wood the route crosses the remains of the Wey & Arun Junction Canal to join the old trackbed of a railway axed in the Beeching cuts. Our route continues along this lovely wooded

Country Walks in Surrey

Distance: 3½ miles

Starting point: Woodhill Lane by the village duck pond.
GR 032438

How to get there: Shamley Green is 4 miles south of
Guildford on the B2128. Park at the roadside in Woodhill
Lane, 100 yards south of the Red Lion Inn.

OS Map: Landranger 186 Aldershot & Guildford

Refreshments: The Red Lion Inn, or picnic along the way.

path that is shared by the Downs Link and the Wey-South paths.
The track forms the halfway point of the circuit and dotted along the
way are seats ideal for a leisurely picnic. After leaving this Arcadian
delight, the route continues along a quiet road that returns you to the
village green.

The Walk

❶ Cross a section of the dissected village green southwards going
between the pond and the B2128 to soon meet a lane. Go ahead
along a short unmade drive and continue on a signed footpath
between the gates of **Mellow House** and **Summer Meadow**.
The narrow fenced path goes between gardens before reaching a
field. Continue ahead up a low rise and turn right through a kissing
gate signed **GW** (Greensand Way) and continue between fields to
pass a church and meet the B2128 road.

❷ Cross the road to a small car park opposite and continue ahead
on a bridleway. The path now passes between open fields

with panoramic views before ending at a lane where our way is leftwards passing **Little Common Cottage**. Keep to a well-trodden path that goes through a bluebell wood and ignore paths to your left. After crossing a stream, maintain direction ahead to join a cart track in 120 yards. Go ahead alongside a field and at its end continue on the track for a few yards where to left and right you will see the remains of the **Wey & Arun Junction Canal**. Some 20 yards before the parapet of a bridge, fork right on a downhill path to meet the old railway trackbed.

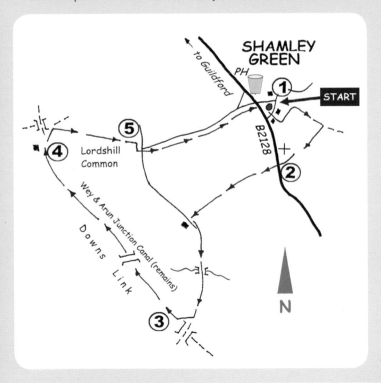

3 Turn right along the wooded track that is a section of the **Downs Link** and **Wey-South** long-distance paths that are also shared by cyclists. Dotted along the way are seats that make ideal picnic spots.

4 After 1 mile, with a house and its large garden to your left and a wooden bridge 20 yards ahead, fork right down a slope to meet a metalled track. Turn right along the track and after crossing a bridge over a stream fork right along a straight path that goes between fields.

5 The path ends at a lane where you should turn right to meet a small road junction in 50 yards. Go left here along the road which will bring you back to the village green. At the green, fork right to meet the B2128 and **Woodhill Lane** opposite to complete this super walk.

Runnymede, Cooper's Hill and the River Thames

■ *The Air Forces Memorial at the top of Cooper's Hill* ■

Distance: 4 miles

Starting point: The National Trust pay and display car park beside the River Thames. GR 997731

How to get there: Runnymede is 1 mile west of Egham and junction 13 of the M25. From the A30 Egham bypass roundabout, take the A308 towards Windsor and 1 mile after passing the Runnymede Pleasure Grounds park in the National Trust car park on the bank of the Thames.

OS Map: Landranger 176 West London

Refreshments: A café in the Runnymede Pleasure Grounds, or picnic along the route.

This splendid walk begins in Runnymede's famous water meadows where King John was forced to sign the Magna Carta in June 1215. The name Runnymede is believed to derive from the Anglo-Saxon *'runieg'* for regular meeting and *'mede'* for mead or meadow. The route soon meets the John F. Kennedy Memorial, a noble block of inscribed Portland stone, before it continues up the slopes of Cooper's Hill. At the top it passes the Air Forces Memorial, a fitting monument to the brave men and women of the Allied Air Forces who died during the Second World War and an intriguing place to visit. After leaving this lofty place, the way returns to the water meadows below and meets the bank of the Thames which it follows to complete this appealing circuit.

The Walk

❶ Cross the A308 via a pedestrian refuge 30 yards west of the car park entrance and go ahead on a grassy path towards a tree line.

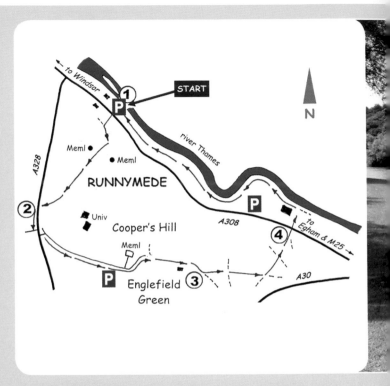

At the tree line, turn left and at a marker post on your right, go right through a kissing gate. Now follow a magical granite sett path between the trees to reach the splendid **John F. Kennedy Memorial**. The route passes the memorial and continues ahead on an unmade path that climbs the slope to meet with a quiet drive which is followed to its end at the A328.

2 Cross the main road and go left along the pavement for a short distance before turning left into **Cooper's Hill Lane**. Follow this

■ *The bank of the Thames makes a great picnic spot* ■

quiet lane to meet the **Air Forces Memorial** that is worthy of a visit. The building, reminiscent of a wartime airfield control tower, was designed by Sir Edward Maufe and the roof-top observation point gives magnificent views over the Thames and far beyond. This inspiring monument contains sculptures by Vernon Hill, engraved glass and painted ceilings by John Hutton and a moving poem on the gallery window by Paul H. Scott. The route continues along the lane that soon bends left and the tarmac surface ends. Go ahead on the track and follow it rightward downhill where it later narrows.

③ Go through a kissing gate on your left at a field edge, cross a meadow and pass through a second gate opposite. Go ahead on an indistinct grassy path through the water meadow with the houses of **Egham** seen ahead in the distance. When a hedgerow comes in from the left, leave this path and follow the hedgerow edge. Later when the hedgerow bends left, continue ahead to a distant stile beside the A308 with an industrial building beyond.

④ Cross the road and continue ahead passing the side of the industrial building to meet the bank of the **Thames**. Our route is now to the left along the water's edge where you soon pass through the **Runnymede Pleasure Grounds** where the riverbank is dotted with seats. To complete this interesting circuit, continue along the riverbank until the car park is reached.

6
Ripley, Pyrford and the Wey Navigation

■ *A narrowboat leaving Walsham Lock* ■

This lovely circuit leaves Ripley Green – believed to be the biggest in Surrey – and soon meets the scenic towpath of the Wey Navigation by Walsham Weir and Lock. During the summer months colourful narrowboats piloted by weekend sailors ply the peaceful waters and negotiate the locks. After

Country Walks in Surrey

Distance: 4 miles

Starting point: Car park on Ripley Green. GR 053571

How to get there: Ripley is off the A3 some 2½ miles south of junction 10 of the M25. When approaching from the A3, turn right on a narrow lane 80 yards after passing the Half Moon pub and park in the designated area on the left after 150 yards.

OS Map: Landrangers 187 Dorking & Reigate and 186 Aldershot & Guildford

Refreshments: The Half Moon pub, or picnic along the way.

following the towpath for a while the way passes through Pyrford Green and crosses fields to meet pretty Pyrford village and its ancient church. After following a road for a short distance, the route rejoins the towpath for the homeward leg where it passes Newark Lock before rejoining our outward path by Walsham Weir from where we return to Ripley Green.

The Walk

❶ Leave the parking area by continuing along the track heading away from the village. At the end of a pair of cottages, follow the track left to soon meet two houses. Here go ahead on a signed path where you cross a bridge and continue between fields to meet with **Walsham Weir**.

❷ Cross the weir and turn right passing **Walsham Lock** and the lock-keeper's cottage. Ignore a bridge on your left and continue along the pretty towpath. As you walk, the **River Wey** will be seen below to your right; testimony of how the locks between here and the **Thames** have raised the height of the canal.

❸ When a bridge is met on your left, cross it and follow a well-trodden path between a large garden and fields to reach a drive. Continue along the drive to meet a road and then go ahead along **Elveden Close** and at its end, continue on a fenced path.

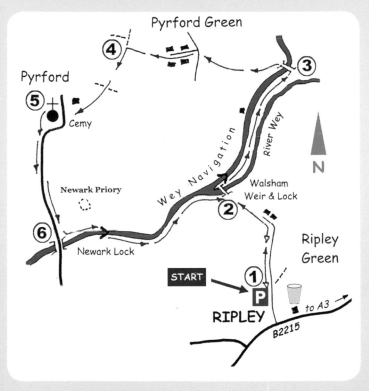

4 The path ends at a stile which you should cross. Now turn left and follow a wide path along the field edge, later ignoring a path to left and right. As you near farm buildings, keep ahead and pass through two pedestrian gates in quick succession. Now continue through a small paddock passing to the left of a house and its garden and cross two stiles in the tree line ahead. Continue ahead on a paved path through a graveyard to meet and cross a road with caution.

5 Go ahead up a grassy slope to the memorial cross by **Pyrford's** ancient church which is well worth investigation. It still retains its Norman doorway and zigzag stone moulding which is protected by a delightful Tudor porch while inside are traces of red ochre wall paintings nearly 900 years old and 15th-century pews. Go ahead to the gates of the **Old Vicarage** and turn left on a downhill path to meet a road. Continue ahead alongside the road passing the stark remains of **Newark Priory** in the water meadows to your left.

6 At traffic lights by a narrow bridge, turn left to rejoin the canal and press on along the towpath. At **Newark Lock** cross a bridge and continue along the opposite bank to reach **Walsham Weir**. Turn

■ *A game of cricket being played on Ripley Green* ■

right here and retrace your steps back to **Ripley Green** and the end of this interesting walk.

7

Cranleigh, the Wey-South and Downs Link paths

■ *Admiring a blaze of colour* ■

Distance: 4½ miles

Starting point: Pay and display car park in Village Way by Cranleigh Leisure Centre. GR 058389

How to get there: Cranleigh is 8 miles south of Guildford on the B2128.

OS Maps: Landranger 186 Aldershot & Guildford and 187 Dorking & Reigate

Refreshments: Cranleigh has many eateries, or picnic along the route.

This is a beautiful walk during springtime when the paths are lined by bluebells, red campion, stitchwort, primroses and orchids. After leaving the bustling village, the route crosses magnificent parkland and for a while follows the Wey-South Path as it passes delightful Uttworth Manor to reach the towpath of the defunct Wey and Arun Junction Canal, a good picnic spot. After leaving the long-distance path, the way continues along an ancient byway and across fields to meet with another, the Downs Link Path where the bed of an old railway line and a haven for wildlife brings us easily back to Cranleigh and the end of this level circuit.

The Walk

❶ From the car park, pass **Cranleigh Leisure Centre** to meet a metalled drive with playing fields beyond. Turn right along this drive to reach a road where you should turn left alongside it. In 70 yards, turn right on a signed public footpath and remain ahead on this scenic path as it leads you through the superb landscape of **Knowle Park**.

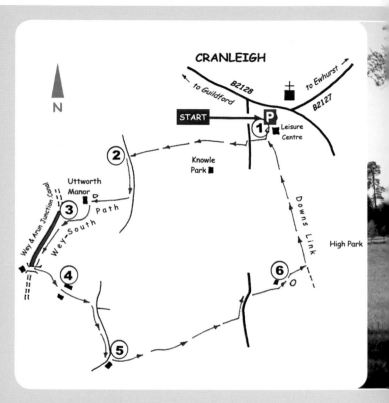

CRANLEIGH

to Guildford · B2128 · to Ewhurst · B2127

N

START

P

① Leisure Centre

② Knowle Park ■

Uttworth Manor

Wey & Arun Junction Canal

③ Path

Wey-South

④

Downs Link

High Park

⑥ O

⑤

❷ The path ends at a lane and here we meet with the **Wey-South Path** which the route follows for the next mile. Turn left along the lane and at a house on your right, go right along a drive leading to 17th-century **Uttworth Manor**. Just before reaching the house and when at the end of a pond on your right, turn left through a gate to enter a field. Follow the path as it swings right and at the corner of the field, turn left beside a hedgerow. Soon go over a bridge on your right that crosses the **River Wey south branch**

■ *Knowle Park* ■

and fork left to meet the towpath of the defunct **Wey & Arun Junction Canal**.

❸ Continue along the towpath. The canal was short-lived due to the coming of the Guildford to Horsham railway which was later closed during Dr Beeching's cuts. Cross a stile beside **Mill Farm** where ahead you will notice the dried-up impression of the canal continuing through a field. Turn left here; cross a bridge over a stream and in 30 yards go ahead through a field gate. Keep ahead, pass through a second gate and press on alongside a hedgerow. When the hedgerow bends right, remain alongside it to meet the corner of the field. Ignore two gates on your right and go ahead through another signed as the **Wey-South Path**.

4 Pass a wooden building to meet a driveway and continue ahead between a bungalow and **Great Garson**, another fine 17th-century house. Go ahead along the drive where primroses, bluebells and orchids grow in spring. When the drive ends at a lane, turn right along it and at a right bend go left on a byway beside **Eastbridge Cottage**.

5 This peaceful byway leads you through a quiet bluebell wood and finally ends at a country lane. Turn left along the lane to soon reach a drive leading to **Pond House** and others on your right. Follow the drive and when at the gate to **Pond House** go left over a stile and pass to the left of a duck pond to cross a second stile.

6 Go ahead along the field edge and in 90 yards turn right between trees and cross a bridge over a brook. Cross the next field to a gap in the tree line opposite to meet the trackbed of a railway line that once linked Guildford to Horsham. This has been adopted as a part of the **Downs Link** long-distance path and is shared by cyclists. Turn left along the trackbed passing a sign indicating that **Cranleigh** is 1½ miles ahead although it is only half that distance to arrive at the **Cranleigh Leisure Centre** and the end of this very pretty walk.

8
Friday Street and Evelyn country

■ *St John's church and the Evelyn Chapel* ■

Country Walks in Surrey

Distance: 3½ miles

Starting point: Friday Street car park. GR 125457

How to get there: From Dorking, follow the A25 west for 3 miles before turning south along Hollow Lane signed to Leith Hill and Friday Street. In 1 mile turn sharp left on a lane signed to Friday Street to meet the car park on your right in ½ mile. There is no parking in the hamlet.

OS Map: Landranger 187 Dorking & Reigate

Refreshments: The Wotton Hatch pub at the mid point of the walk, or picnic along the way.

This wonderful walk begins amid the beauty of Friday Street, a small hamlet set beside a picturesque hammer pond. The pretty circuit passes through a landscape which influenced John Evelyn whose famous book *Sylva – A Discourse Of Forest Trees* was published in 1664. He was a prolific author and good friend of Samuel Pepys but is probably best known for the extensive diaries he kept throughout his long life. After passing between pretty fields with fish pools strung out like a string of pearls, the route skirts the grounds of Evelyn's house in Wotton from where a small excursion takes you to St John's church and the Evelyn Chapel. The return route is along a fine bridleway that brings you to the hamlet of Broadmoor from where it is but a short walk back to the hammer pond.

The Walk

❶ Leave the car park on a downhill path beside the road to meet the pretty hammer pond. Turn left down a track and immediately pass **Pond Cottage**, cross a small ford and at **Yew Tree Cottage**

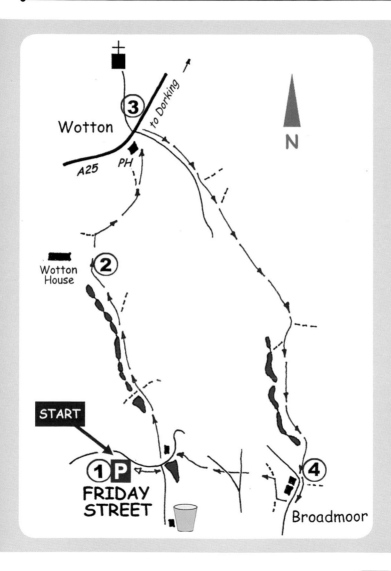

fork left. At a junction of paths beside a pond and stone bridge, go ahead over a stile and continue on this wonderful track later ignoring a footpath forking right. The quiet walker stands every chance of spotting a roe deer grazing in this idyllic valley.

2 After rounding a bend, go down a small slope and fork left down steps to reach a meadow. Cross a stile and pass through the meadow to meet a driveway. John Evelyn's **Wotton House** is set in this sylvan paradise to your left. Turn right along the splendid drive and after rounding a bend and before another, cross a stile on your right and go diagonally left across a meadow to reach **Wotton village hall** and enter a car park. Go ahead through the car park to the A25 and the splendid **Wotton Hatch pub**. Opposite is a small lane leading to **St John's church** and the **Evelyn Chapel** where a small excursion there and back will add a further ½ mile.

3 The way turns sharply right here and continues along **Sheephouse Lane**. Pass a small housing development at **Sheephouse Green** and 100 yards later, on a right bend, fork left to pass the side of a cottage. Immediately after passing the cottage fork left and follow a cart track. When this soon enters a field go ahead on a narrower track. Now remain on this track for almost 1¼ miles ignoring side paths until it finally ends at a lane beside stables in **Broadmoor**.

4 Go ahead along the lane passing a couple of pretty cottages and at the gate to **Leith Cottage**, turn right on a footpath that soon ends at a T-junction. Now turn right up a slope and at a marker post on a bend, turn left up a narrow path through woodland. When the path is joined by another from the right, continue left to reach a lane. Go ahead on a path opposite and maintain direction at a second lane. The way now descends through magnificent woodland and finally reaches the bank of **Friday Street's** hammer pond. Cross the dam and retrace your earlier path back to the car park and the end of the walk.

■ *The scenic hammer pond at Friday Street* ■

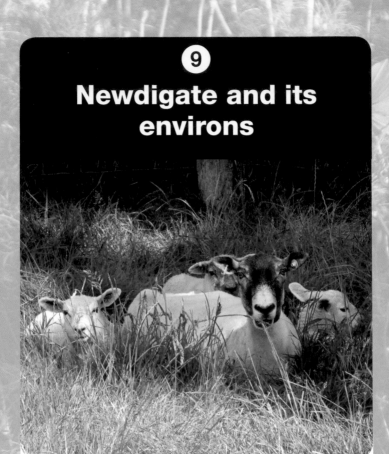

9

Newdigate and its environs

■ Sheltering from the midday sun ■

This charming walk is set deep in the Surrey Weald and utilizes a good variety of farm drives, cart tracks and field paths lined by pretty hedgerows and pastoral scenery. Beginning beside St Peter's church with its wooden tower supported by timbers hewn from the Weald 500 years ago, the route follows

Distance: 3½ miles

Starting point: Beside St Peter's church in Church Lane. GR 198421

How to get there: Newdigate is 2 miles east of Beare Green and the A24 south of Dorking. Church Lane is at the southern end of the village.

OS Map: Landranger 187 Dorking & Reigate

Refreshments: The Six Bells pub opposite St Peter's church.

a quiet lane that leads to a very pleasant farm track offering easy walking and expansive views. The way turns west when Home Farm is reached and continues along its driveway to meet with field paths. Soon the circuit turns again and heads for Greens Farm as it begins its return. After following the farm drive that offers panoramic views, the way finally crosses pretty fields to rejoin the village.

The Walk

❶ With your back to the **Six Bells pub**, walk along **Church Lane** passing the converted buildings of **Dean House Farm** and a roadside pond. At a junction with **Hogspudding Lane**, turn right along **Cudworth Lane**. When this bends left by the entrance to **Green Lane Farm**, go ahead along the farm drive signed as a bridleway.

❷ Pass **Green Lane Farm Cottage** and continue ahead between barns where the way now follows a cart track. Ignore a crossing path and continue ahead along the bridleway. At the end of woodland, go through a gate and continue alongside a field where you pass low barns before going through a second gate to meet the drive of **Home Farm** in 12 yards.

❸ Turn right along the farm drive soon passing the gates of **The Bungalow**. Some 10 yards after passing the gate of **Ockley Lodge**, turn right over a stile and cross a small paddock to meet a pedestrian gate. Now continue through a second paddock to meet and cross a stile in the far right corner and go out to a road.

❹ Turn left along the road and 30 yards later turn right on a signed bridleway along a field edge passing through pedestrian gates along the way. At a field gate by a brook, continue ahead and look out for a stile and fingerpost on your right. Turn right here and follow an indistinct path crossing a bridge in 65 yards. Now follow the left side of a field and cross a stile in the top left corner. Here maintain direction along the right side of a field that leads to the buildings of **Greens Farm**. Ignore a stile on your right and continue along the hedgerow passing barns before finally crossing a stile and going ahead to meet a low brick building.

■ *St Peter's church* ■

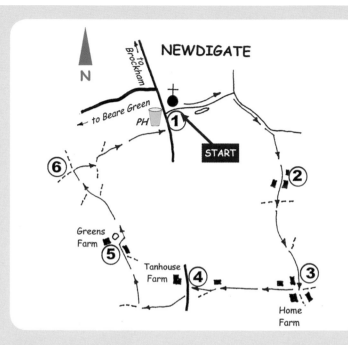

5 Turn right here, pass a duck pond and at a junction of tracks turn left. Soon ignore a couple of tracks to your left and remain on the farm drive. Later, ignore a signed path to your right on a bend and a second to the left 80 yards later.

6 At the beginning of woodland on your left, turn right over two stiles in quick succession and enter a field. Follow the right side and cross a stile in the corner to meet a T-junction of paths. Go left here and follow the left-hand field edge. Ignore a path on your left and press on alongside the next couple of fields to meet a road where 100 yards to your left is **St Peter's church** and the end of this fine circuit.

⑩
Brockham, the Pilgrims' Way and old quarry workings

■ *Far-reaching views can be enjoyed from the path* ■

This circuit is a must for those who enjoy wild flora and fauna. After leaving Brockham, the route follows an old coach road between fields to reach the A25. From here the way heads for the lower slopes of Box Hill where it continues through fields with panoramic views and joins up with the Pilgrims' Way where an area of old quarry workings is passed that is now a Site of Special Scientific Interest (SSSI). After leaving the Pilgrims' Way, the route continues over fields and along quiet lanes to cross the River Mole and rejoin the village green.

Country Walks in Surrey

Distance: 4 miles

Starting point: Wheelers Lane beside Christ Church, Brockham. GR 197494

How to get there: Brockham is off the A25, 1½ miles east of Dorking. Follow the signs to the village centre.

OS Map: Landranger 187 Dorking & Reigate

Refreshments: The Duke's Head and the Royal Oak both face Brockham village green, or picnic along the route.

The Walk

1 Walk to the ancient wellhead on the village green and then go along **Old School Lane**. Soon after crossing a brook, fork right on a signed bridleway along an old coaching road. After passing between the fairways of a golf club, a tarmac drive is met. Continue ahead along the drive and turn right to meet the A25 main road.

2 The route continues along the lane opposite, but it is safer to cross at the pedestrian refuge 70 yards to your right. Pass between the car parks of a garden centre and cross a footbridge over the **River Mole**; the road bridge was swept away many years ago during a flood. Now follow the quiet lane, ignore a road on your right and later pass under a railway bridge.

3 Some 30 yards after going under power cables, go right over a stile by a **National Trust Box Hill Farm sign** and enter a large field. Cross the field following the line of power cables to reach a stile at the far side. Go ahead to meet a T-junction and then turn right along the **Pilgrims' Way** beside a line of yew trees. The path is believed to be Neolithic but it was the Victorian mapmakers who romantically named it. Pass through two kissing gates in quick succession ignoring a crossing bridleway.

❹ Soon after passing a line of quarry workers' cottages seen through the trees on your right, a broad track joins from the left. A short excursion leftwards here brings you to a fascinating SSSI below the high chalk cliffs of the defunct quarry where many butterflies and wildflowers will be seen during the summer months. After investigating these workings or maybe picnicking, return to this spot and resume your original direction to meet a clearing with an information board by the ruins of limekilns. Follow the path around

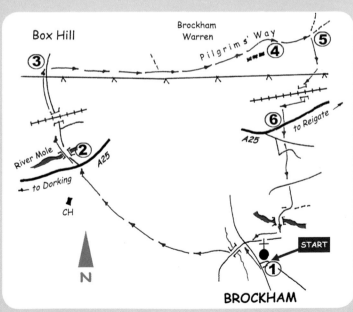

the right side of the kilns and press on along the **Pilgrims' Way** to meet a junction of paths by a directional post.

5 Turn right over a stile and cross a field towards a marker post 50 yards to the right of a pylon. From the marker post, go diagonally right to the field corner and cross a stile. Go left under a railway bridge and then immediately right on a well-trodden signed path along a field edge. Look out for a marker post and a stile on your left which you should cross. Now press on through the centre of the field following a line of power cables to rejoin the A25.

■ *Brockham's pretty village green* ■

6 Cross the road with caution and go ahead on a footpath to meet and cross a smaller road where you should continue along unmade **Mill Hill Lane**. Cross another road and press on ahead before finally meeting a marker post beside a garden. Follow the lane rightwards downhill to meet and cross a footbridge over the **River Mole**. Continue on a tarmac path to reach the village pound where a right turn brings you to the village green with **Christ Church** to your left and the end of this great circuit.

11

Banstead Wood and the fields of Perrotts Farm

■ *The scenic driveway of Perrotts Farm* ■

This super figure-of-eight walk begins with a short sharp hill but the small effort required is well rewarded by gently undulating countryside that is about as remote as one can get when so near south London's suburbia. The circuit begins in

Distance: 4½ miles

Starting point: Banstead Wood car park off Holly Lane, Banstead. GR 273583

How to get there: From the western end of Banstead High Street, go south on Bolters Lane (B2217) and soon continue ahead along Holly Lane (B2219) for 2½ miles to meet the car park just before the junction with Outwood Lane (B2032).

OS Map: Landranger 187 Dorking & Reigate

Refreshments: There are coffee shops and eateries in Banstead High Street, or picnic among the trees.

Banstead Wood that is a joy at any time of the year but is at its very best during late April when the bluebells are in bloom. After emerging from the woodland beside Perrotts Farm, the way follows the farm drive with panoramic views before crossing fields to circle Ruffett Wood. More scenic paths follow as the circuit makes its return to Banstead Wood where wide paths through the majestic woodland bring you easily to the end of this really good circuit.

The Walk

❶ Leave the car park via a kissing gate opposite the vehicle exit and go up a slope alongside a line of yew trees before turning right through a kissing gate. Here you should follow the left fork uphill for a short distance to meet a welcome seat. Turn right here along a wide level path and ignore side paths. The path eventually goes down a dip and bends right to meet a junction of paths with the buildings of **Park Farm** just beyond the trees on your right.

■ *A pastoral view along the way* ■

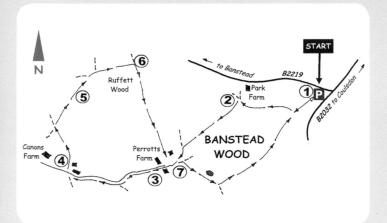

2 Turn left at this junction and continue on a stony rising path until it finally ends at a T-junction with the buildings of **Perrotts Farm** seen through the trees ahead. Go left now and zigzag between trees to meet a fork. Take the right fork towards a field and when a path enters from the left, press on and follow it as it bends right ignoring a stile in the field edge. Pass through a kissing gate beside a barn and turn left to pass the farmhouse to reach the farm drive.

3 Now follow the drive as it leads you between fields with panoramic views. During winter when the hedgerow on your right is denuded of its leaves, the lichen *Xanthoria parientina* provides a wonderfully vivid display.

4 Some 50 yards after passing a pair of white-painted cottages, turn right on a signed footpath and soon cross a stile. Now follow a hedgerow along the left field edge until a crossing path and directional post is met. Turn right here and cross the field to reach another post at the far side by the woodland edge. Pass through a kissing gate and continue through trees to meet with a large field.

5 Turn left along the field edge and soon pass through a kissing gate beside a tall pine tree. Continue ahead between trees and ignore a path on your left. After emerging at another large field, keep ahead and ignore a path on your left. Press on along the perimeter of **Ruffett Wood** until the curving path ends at a T-junction with a field ahead of you.

6 Now turn right and follow a well-trodden rising path alongside fields as it leads you back to **Perrotts Farm**. Continue through the kissing gate that you passed through earlier beside the barn and follow the path as it soon swings away from the field, ignoring a left fork in 15 yards.

7 Keep ahead to re-enter **Banstead Wood** and in 90 yards when the path is about to pass between two tall oak trees by a seat, turn right and continue along a level track where you pass an ideal picnic spot beside a woodland pool. Some 70 yards beyond this pool when the track divides, follow the left fork. Now remain on this wide track as it gradually leads you downhill to meet with your outward path and the car park where the walk began.

■ *The 15th-century Brewerstreet Farmhouse* ■

This interesting walk is steeped in history. Beginning in Bletchingley, a village well known for its antique shops, the route soon passes an ancient church before crossing fields with panoramic views. After turning west, the circuit passes by the hamlet of Brewer Street and a magnificent timber-framed

Country Walks in Surrey

Distance: 3¾ miles

Starting point: A service road beside the A25, 150 yards west of the Red Lion pub. GR 323507

How to get there: Bletchingley is on the A25 between Redhill and Godstone. The service road is at the western end of the village.

OS Map: Landranger 187 Dorking & Reigate

Refreshments: The Red Lion pub near the beginning of the circuit.

house some 600 years old. Following level paths, the way meets the turning point at Pendell and passes more historic houses before joining a gently rising path alongside fields that all too soon ends back at the village.

The Walk

❶ From the service road, walk east towards the village and pass the **Red Lion pub** to reach **Stychens Lane**. Turn left down the lane and when it forks, turn right on a path beside a house named **Old**

■ *Taking in the view* ■

Works. Now continue ahead on a pleasant path with far-reaching views to arrive at the graveyard of **St Mary's church**. The way is ahead to meet **Church Lane**, but by passing to the right of the church you will see a quaint corner of the village and the remains of a hermit's cell in the south wall of the church.

2 Turn left along **Church Lane** and when opposite the entrance to **Bletchingley Golf Club**, turn left on a signed footpath. After passing a low brick wall on your left, turn right over a stile and go ahead alongside a fairway ignoring crossing paths. Keep close to the hedgerow on your left and when it swings rightwards, go left on a well-trodden path between trees to reach and cross a stile at a field edge.

3 Cross the centre of the field to meet a lane at the far side and then turn left along it until a T-junction is met. Along the way on your right, take a peek up the drive to **Place Farm** where the remains of the gateway to **Anne of Cleves' house** is imbedded in the front wall of the early 18th-century farmhouse. Turn left at a T-junction and continue along **Brewer Street**. Just before a building is met on your right, turn right on a farm drive and pass the side of 15th-century **Brewerstreet Farmhouse**. Continue along the left side of a large barn and then follow a very pleasant bridleway between fields with magnificent views.

4 At a driveway to **The Hawthorns School**, keep ahead and pass an eclectic group of buildings where a left fork brings you to a country road. Turn left along the road and pass the impressive Jacobean frontage of the school built in 1624 and formerly known as **Pendell Court**. Continue along the road passing **Pendell House** by Inigo Jones, on your right, that dates from 1636. Pass a small lake and **Pendell Manor House** (built in 1730) on your left and at the end of its garden wall, turn left over a stile to enter a field.

⑤ Go directly across the centre of the field aiming for a house in the distance. After crossing the widest part of the field, maintain direction alongside a hedgerow to meet and cross a stile beside a field gate to soon join a country lane. Ignore a stile ahead of you and continue ahead on the lane passing the **Old Rectory**, a beautiful building dating from 1786.

⑥ At a left bend by cottages, turn right on a pretty path that climbs easily back towards **Bletchingley**. At the entrance to **Dormers Farm**, go ahead on a path above and beside the drive to rejoin the house named **Old Works** where you should now retrace your steps back to the A25 where on your right is the **Red Lion** and, beyond, the end of this interesting circuit.

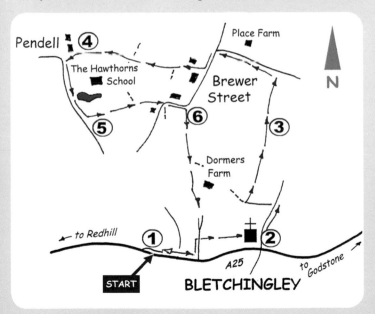

⑬ Lingfield and the fields of Park Farm

■ *Lingfield's old lock-up lies in the shade of an ancient oak* ■

This varied and interesting walk explores the old village of Lingfield as well as the pretty fields of Park Farm. After leaving the village cage, where unruly locals once spent the night to await daylight and soberness, the way continues along the High Street before meeting with the fields of Park Farm. Easily-

Distance: 2½ miles

Starting point: Car park off Gun Pit Road. GR 385435

How to get there: Lingfield is 2¼ miles south-east of the A22 at Blindley Heath. Gun Pit Road is at the centre of the village opposite the village cage.

OS Map: Landranger 187 Dorking & Reigate

Refreshments: Several eateries in the High Street.

followed paths with lovely views lead you through a timeless Wealden landscape before returning you to a quiet corner of the village. Here, 16th-century houses in Church Approach and the ancient church of St Peter and St Paul are passed before the way rejoins the bustling High Street of this lovely village.

The Walk

1 Go out of the car park entrance and turn right to meet the **High Street**. Cross the road to the village cage that was last used as a lock-up in 1882, and turn right alongside the road. Later cross the end of **Old School Place** and continue alongside the road. Turn left into **Church Road** and at the end of the car park of the **Star pub**, go right on a public footpath between fields.

2 The footpath ends beside **New Place**, a large stone house built in 1617 and here you should turn right alongside the road. When at the gateway to **Brook House** on your left, turn left on a fenced path that leads to **Lingfield railway station** where you should heed the **Stop, Look and Listen sign** before crossing the tracks to meet open fields. Go ahead and soon cross a bridge over a

LINGFIELD

to Blindley Heath

B2029

Park Farm

(4)

(5)

Stn

PH

(2)

(3)

B2028

to Edenbridge

to Newchapel

(1) P

START

N

■ *The path outside the village* ■

stream. Keep ahead over the next field and cross a second bridge and fork right to pass through a kissing gate.

❸ Now press on along a broad path beside oak trees and when climbing a slight rise, look out for directional arrows on a post to your right. Here turn left and continue through the centre of a large arable field to meet a line of trees ahead. Pass through the trees and continue ahead through the next field with a hedgerow on your right. When this hedgerow bends right, fork diagonally left across the field and aim to the right of a bungalow.

❹ From the bungalow, go ahead along a cart track to meet a T-junction with the buildings of **Park Farm** to your right. Turn left along a track that leads you back to the railway line that you should cross, heeding the warning sign, and go ahead to a road. Turn left along the road for a few yards before turning right along **Baker's Lane**.

❺ At a road junction, turn left along **Church Road** to soon meet our outward path beside the **Star public house**. Turn sharp right here along **Church Approach**, the oldest corner of the village. The plain brick cottages on your right were built around 1700 and once contained the original Star Inn. Fork left alongside the church and fork left again to continue on a fenced footpath. At **Old School Place** go ahead to rejoin the **High Street** where you should turn right and retrace your steps back to the car park to complete this good walk.

■ *The highest point on the route is reached under a dramatic sky* ■

Country Walks in Surrey

This enchanting walk begins by following the Vanguard Way long-distance path that leads you easily to the highest point of the circuit at Nore Hill on the North Downs where, on a clear day, all the main features of our capital city can be spotted. As the way turns west it descends into Halliloo Valley and for a short distance follows a quiet road that brings you to the fairways of Woldingham Golf Club. The route circles the picturesque grounds before making its way out of the valley on a climb that should not trouble the average person. The track offers far-reaching views over the valley before meeting with a level path that returns you to Chelsham to complete this exhilarating walk.

The Walk

❶ From the approach road, pass the front of the **Bull Inn** and continue over the common to reach a road. Turn left along the wide strip of grass beside the road passing a small pond to meet a road junction. Turn right, pass through a gate and continue on a track signed as a bridleway. The track continues alongside fields and ends at a lane in just over ½ mile.

❷ Turn right along the lane to soon meet the B269. Turn right alongside the B269 for 80 yards before crossing it and seeking out a signed footpath to the left of gated **Baynards Road**. The

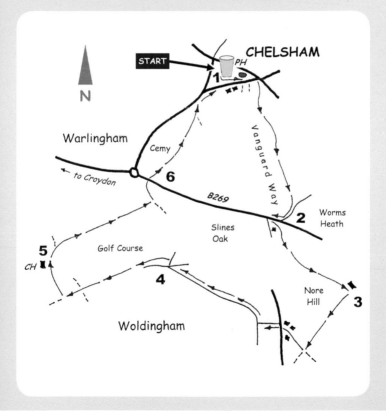

path skirts a garden before passing through woodland and ending at a stile at a field edge. Cross the stile and go ahead passing to the left of a deep depression. Continue across the field aiming just to the right of a house in the distance.

3 Turn right here alongside a hedgerow and soon descend into **Halliloo Valley** where a wide track lined by an avenue of trees is met. So far you have been following a section of the 68-mile-long **Vanguard Way** that begins in London and ends at Seaford on the coast, but here we leave it by turning right along the track where we soon pass an eclectic group of farm buildings to reach a road. Cross the road and continue ahead on an unmade track opposite. At a T-junction, turn right and now follow a pleasant residential road until it ends at **Halliloo Valley Road**.

4 Cross the road and continue ahead along unmade **High Lane** for 40 yards before turning left through a gate and following a bridleway that skirts the fairways of **Woldingham Golf Club**. When the golf club drive is met, turn right alongside it on the bridleway and pass the front of the club house.

5 Continue between the 1st and 13th tees where the track soon goes uphill and forks. Follow the right fork and remain on this track as it climbs steadily out of the valley and finally ends at a T-junction. Turn left here and follow a wide track that soon ends at the B269.

6 Cross the B269 and go ahead along **Rogers Lane** opposite. Some 20 yards after passing a livery stable, keep left at a fork and follow this path through woodland until it ends at a road. Turn right alongside the road to meet **Chelsham Common** where you go ahead towards the **Bull Inn** to complete this excellent walk.

■ *On the path to Woldingham* ■

Moorhouse and The High Chart

■ *The Carpenters Arms marks the halfway point* ■

Distance: 3¼ miles

Starting point: Car park in Moorhouse Road. GR 430529

How to get there: Moorhouse is on the A25 and 2 miles east of Limpsfield. Moorhouse Road is off the A25 opposite the car park of the Grasshopper Inn. The car park will be found on your right after just over ¼ mile.

OS Map: Landranger 187 Dorking & Reigate

Refreshments: The Carpenters Arms at the halfway point, or picnic along the route.

This enjoyable pastoral walk begins by following the woodland edge before turning south and heading for The High Chart on a barely perceptible climb through fields with panoramic views. After joining the Greensand Way long-distance path and passing the halfway point at Limpsfield Chart, the route then immerses itself in the superb National Trust woodland of The High Chart where quiet paths lead through this densely forested area. When the route meets with the Kent border it turns, leaves the long-distance path and begins an easy descent through the trees to complete the circuit.

The Walk

❶ From a **National Trust sign** at the end of the car park, go right on a path alongside a large circular grassy area. When about halfway around, turn right through trees and go down an incline to meet a T-junction at a field edge. Turn left and follow this path along the woodland edge with fields on your right. When a gate across the path is met, pass through it and go ahead over a meadow. Continue through a gate opposite and press on along the woodland edge.

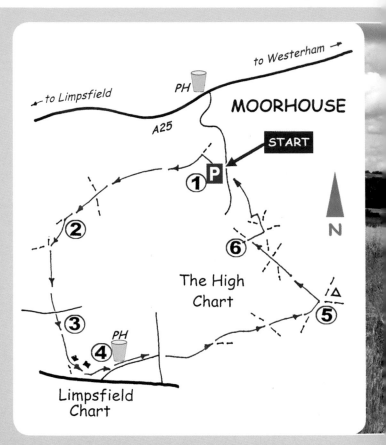

2 When nearing the end of the woodland, pass a waymarker and 10 yards later turn left on a narrow path to meet and cross a stile in 25 yards. Cross a narrow field to meet a cart track and then turn left along the slowly rising track. Cross a stile beside a field gate ahead of you and continue on the track to meet with a road.

■ *Along the way* ■

❸ Cross the road and go ahead on a signed bridleway opposite that crosses a field. Just before a house is met, turn right through a hedgerow and follow a gravel drive passing **Lombarden Farm** and a barn conversion before forking left along the drive to meet with a road. Turn left alongside the road on a path that soon meets with a country lane. Go ahead on a track opposite signed **GW** (Greensand Way) that soon bends right to meet the **Carpenters Arms pub** and the halfway point of the circuit at **Limpsfield Chart**.

4 Turn left alongside the road to meet a T-junction and go ahead on the signed **GW** path opposite. After 250 yards look out for a **GW** marker post where you should fork left and then follow the well-marked **GW** path until the Kent border is met at a junction of tracks marked by a stone cairn topped by a **Greensand Way distance marker**.

5 Here, leave the long-distance path and, 5 yards before a water tank, turn sharp left and follow a straight path back through the woodland. Keep ahead at a fork and in 120 yards ignore a path to the left and 70 yards later go over a crossing track soon ignoring a signed path on your right.

6 At a second broad crossing track with a downward slope ahead of you, turn right and 80 yards later at marker post, turn left. In 40 yards by a marker post, ignore paths forking left and right and go ahead on the path signed as the **Tandridge Border Path**. Go downhill between pine trees on an indistinct path and keep ahead over a crossing path and low bank to meet another **Tandridge Border Path** marker post. Turn left here for 12 yards before turning right by a second marker post and keep ahead between trees to soon join a gravel drive where a left turn brings you to the car park and the end of this good walk.